GW01182349

KS2
Success
SATs

Level 5

English

LEARN AND PRACTISE

Alison Head

Contents

Speaking and listening

Speaking and listening skills 4

Reading

The language of books 6

Fiction and non-fiction 8

Reading skills 10

Authors and narrators 12

Life stories 14

Writing

Sentences 16

Contractions 18

Possessive apostrophes 20

Punctuation 22

Writing about speech 24

Nouns and pronouns 26

Plurals 28

Adjectives 30

Verbs 32

Adverbs 34

Synonyms 36

Imagery 38

Special effects 40

Instructions 42

Persuasive writing 44

Recounts 46

Reports 48

Planning stories 50

Characters and settings 52

Poetry 54

Glossary

Glossary 56

Answers

Answer booklet (detach from centre of book) 1–4

Speaking and listening skills

Planning for talking

Whether you have been asked to make a presentation on a topic, or take part in a debate, you need to plan what you want to say and think about how you will present your ideas.

Organise your information in a sensible order, then jot down notes to prompt you when you talk. Using prompts sounds more natural than reading the whole thing out like a script.

Practise speaking aloud, to make sure you are speaking slowly and loudly enough.

 Think about the questions you might be asked by the audience and plan how you will respond.

Debating

Debating is all about listening to the views of others and putting your own views across. You may be asked to argue in favour of, or against, a particular idea.

Listen carefully to what people say and jot down anything you disagree with, so you can talk about it when it is your turn to speak. Good debaters reply concisely to the views of their opponents, so that the audience will feel that they have the stronger argument.

Opinions

We all have our own opinions and quite often we form them by listening to what other people say. When someone is speaking, think about whether you agree. Does what they say confirm your opinion, or make you change your mind?

When it is your turn to speak, think about what you could say to convince your listeners to change their opinion.

 Key words opinion

Planning for talking

Think about your speaking and listening skills. Rate your performance in the following areas by underlining the best option.

1   I speak too quickly.   always   sometimes   never

2   I speak too quietly.   always   sometimes   never

3   I have lots of good opinions.   always   sometimes   never

4   I don't speak out when other
    people are talking.   always   sometimes   never

4

Debating

Imagine you have been asked to debate this question: should children be allowed to cycle to school? List three ideas you could use in favour of the idea.

1   _____

2   _____

3   _____

3

Opinions

Read these quotes. Write a sentence about whether or not you agree and why.

1   "It's cruel to make animals perform in a circus."

    _____

2   "Children watch too much TV."

    _____

3   "School children should be allowed to eat whatever they like at lunchtime."

    _____

3

The language of books

The features of books

The features of books are all designed to help you to choose and use books.

Feature	Where is it?	What is it for?
Name of the author	On the cover and inside.	Tells readers who wrote the book.
Name of the publisher	On the cover and inside.	Says the name of the company who made and marketed the book.
ISBN	On the back cover.	Allows shops and libraries to identify the book.
Glossary	At the back of the book.	Alphabetical list of technical words and their definitions.
The blurb	On the back cover.	Gives a glimpse of what is inside the book to attract the reader.

The choices publishers make

All of the features you find in books are put there deliberately by authors and publishers to help the book appeal to the audience it has been written for.

For example, the information books you read might have a glossary to help you with new words. They may have information presented in boxes or bullet points to make it easy to read.

Adult non-fiction books are likely to have a lot more content and use more specialist words.

Top Tip *If you are asked to say why you think a piece of text has certain features, remember that they have been put there on purpose, either to attract readers or to help them to read the text.*

 Key words   author   ISBN   glossary   blurb

The features of books

Fill in the gaps to complete this piece of writing about the features of books.

The covers of books include the name of the writer, or _____,
of the book as well as the name of the publisher. The back carries the
_____, which is the book's unique identifying number.
Inside, the _____ lists the chapters or sections in the book,
while the index lists the topics alphabetically to help readers find what
they need. The _____ lists useful or difficult words and is
found at the back of some books.

4

The choices publishers make

1   Write a sentence to explain why a publisher might present some information
    as bullet points.

    _____

    _____

2   Write a sentence to explain why some information is presented in boxes.

    _____

    _____

3   Why do writers and publishers sometimes include a glossary in non-fiction
    books?

    _____

    _____

3

TOTAL MARKS   7

Fiction and non-fiction

Reading fiction

Fiction authors use their imagination to tell made-up stories, although they could be based on a real person or an event that actually happened.

Fiction for older children and adults is not usually illustrated. Instead, the author uses detailed description and special techniques to create a picture for the reader.

> The chilly wind ran icy fingers through bare winter branches.

When you are reading fiction, especially in a test, look out for how the writer uses these techniques and be ready to comment on how they build up a picture.

 Top Tip *You will find out about different creative writing techniques and how to use them later in the book.*

Reading non-fiction

Non-fiction writing is designed to give information and is packed full of facts. Information is organised into chapters and sections, so readers can find what they need without reading the whole book.

Books are often split into chapters on different subjects. Topics are also listed alphabetically in the index, so readers know exactly where to look.

Non-fiction is often richly illustrated, with pictures, photographs, charts and diagrams all helping to explain the information. Sections of text may be presented as bullet points or put into separate boxes to make it quicker and easier to read.

In a test, think about what kind of non-fiction writing you are reading and make a note of how the information is organised on the page. How does this help the reader?

Scotland
Edinburgh
Newcastle-Upon-Tyne
Pennines
Leeds
Wales
London
Cardiff

 Key words   fiction   non-fiction

Reading fiction

Choose a fiction book that you have read. Find a sentence in which the author has used descriptive language to help you to imagine what a person or place looks like. Copy it out neatly here.

_____

_____

_____

_____

1

Reading non-fiction

Now have a look at a non-fiction book. Tick each of these features when you find them.

A picture caption, to explain what is in a picture. ☐

A photograph. ☐

Information presented in bullet points. ☐

Information in a box. ☐

An index. ☐

5

TOTAL MARKS 6

9

Reading skills

Reading techniques

We need to be able to find information in writing so that we can answer questions in reading comprehension tests.

Skim through the piece of writing quickly to begin with. Think about whether the text is fiction or non-fiction and what it is about. Also, look out for how the text is organised.

Next, read the questions carefully and think about what information you need to answer them. **Scan** through the text again to find key words like the name of a person or place, or a date.

Some questions ask for your opinion. They might ask you what you think about a subject, or what you think the writer feels. You need to read the text carefully again and always back up your answer with evidence.

 If you need to find a date or name, make sure you have found the right one, as there may be more than one!

Top Tip

Using deduction

Sometimes, the answer to a question might not be obvious at first. You might need to read the text again really carefully and think hard about the question. Looking for clues like this is called **deduction**. Also try to imagine how you would feel if you were a character in the story, or the writer of the text. This is called **empathy**.

When you think you have the answer, make sure you back up your opinion with evidence from the text.

 Key words   skim   scan   deduction   empathy

LEARN

READING

Reading techniques

Use your reading skills to answer the questions about this piece of writing.

Holidaymakers visiting Seaward this summer will be surprised to find their view of the beachfront obscured by the latest 'improvement' to the town centre. The new 10-screen cinema opened in March and has, since then, shown films on fewer than half of its screens. Despite its apparent lack of success, the venue's customers have caused traffic chaos on several occasions and one can only imagine how much worse it will be in peak season. Those of us who remember Seaward as a tasteful, sleepy resort are less than impressed.

1 Is the writing fiction or non-fiction? _____

2 What is it about? _____

_____

3 What is the name of the town? _____

4 Why does the writer think that the traffic chaos will be worse in peak season?

_____

_____

4

Using deduction

Read the text again and answer these questions.

1 Do you think the writer is young or old? Explain your answer.

_____

2 Suggest one reason for the writer's opinion on the new development. Provide evidence for your idea from the text.

_____

_____

2

TOTAL MARKS 6

Authors and narrators

LEARN

READING

Authors

Authors are writers. Fiction authors often have their own personal style. Some often write about similar topics, like animal stories or action adventures. Others write on a variety of topics but use a similar format such as diary entries.

If you really enjoy a book, find out if the author has written any others.

If you find an author whose books you love, make sure you tell your friends!

I love Anthony Horowitz!

Jacqueline Wilson is great!

Top Tip *Your local library will be able to find out about books an author has written and get hold of copies for you to read.*

Narrator and viewpoint

The storyteller in a piece of fiction is called the **narrator** and we read things from their **viewpoint**.

Narrators who are not part of the story can tell the reader things that none of the characters know. This can help to build suspense because the reader waits to find out how the characters will react to unfolding events.

When the narrator is a character in the story, the reader gets to know them really well and will be keen to find out what happens to them.

When they choose their narrator, authors also think about how much they want their reader to know at various points in the story.

For example, we know that Cinderella is the beautiful woman at the ball long before the prince does. If the prince were the narrator, we wouldn't know very much about her until he slips the glass slipper onto her foot. How would this affect the story?

Key words   narrator   viewpoint

Authors

1 Think about two books that you have read that are written by the same author. Write down two things that are similar about them. Are they about similar subjects? Are they for the same age group? Are the stories similar in a different way?

a _____

_____

b _____

_____

2 Which book did you prefer? Give a reason for your answer.

_____

_____

3

Narrator and viewpoint

Think again about the well-known story of Cinderella. Write a short paragraph of three sentences about the ball, with one of the ugly sisters as the narrator. Remember that the sisters did not know that Cinders was at the ball!

_____

_____

_____

_____

_____

_____

3

TOTAL MARKS 6

Life stories

Biography

A **biography** is the life story of a person that is written by someone else.

Often, biographies are written about historical figures that people today would like to know more about.

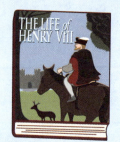

Biographies are written in the **third person**. That means the author is writing about the life of someone else and focuses on what he or she does.

> **She** studied art at college before opening **her** own studio.

Biography is non-fiction and writers research their subjects carefully to get the facts right. Even so, the writer will choose which facts to include and which to leave out, so a biography can never give a complete picture of someone's life.

Autobiography

Autobiographies are life stories written by the person whose story they tell. They are written in the **first person**, so the words show that the writer is telling his or her own story.

> **I** hated **my** itchy brown school uniform and dreamed of being able to choose what **I** wore.

Autobiography is non-fiction but because the author chooses which events to write about and which to leave out, it may not give an entirely accurate picture, especially as our recollection of events may change over time.

 Using the first person can be very effective because it makes the reader feel that the person they are finding out about is speaking directly to them.

 Key words   biography   third person   autobiography   first person

Biography

Answer these questions about biographies.

1 Biographies are written in the third person. Why is this?

_____

_____

_____

2 Does a biography give a complete account of someone's life? Explain your answer.

_____

_____

_____

_____

2

Autobiography

1 What effect does using the first person have on readers of autobiographies?

_____

_____

2 Think of someone you admire, whose autobiography you would like to read. Write down **three** things you would like to find out about them from their autobiography.

a _____

b _____

c _____

_____

4

Sentences

Sentence types

A **sentence** is a group of words that work together. Within sentences, **clauses** contain a **verb** and a **subject**. A subject is the person or thing that does the action.

Simple sentences contain one clause.

Sam bought some trainers.

    subject   verb

Compound sentences are made when two clauses with equal importance are joined together with a special type of word called a **conjunction**.

Jo let the balloon go and it drifted into the sky.

    clause 1   conjunction   clause 2

Complex sentences are built around a **main clause** that would make sense on its own. Added to it is one or more less important clauses, called **subordinate clauses**. They would not make sense on their own.

Joe did his homework while he ate his tea.

    main clause   subordinate clause

Top Tip *Sometimes a subordinate clause is embedded in the middle of a sentence, e.g. My auntie, **who lives in Spain**, sent me a birthday card.*

Using sentence types

When you write, aim to use a variety of sentence types. Too many simple sentences make reading hard work, because the reader must pause every time they reach a full stop. They can be great for drawing attention to important bits in your writing though.

Compound and complex sentences allow you to combine ideas in different ways. The reader does not have to keep pausing for full stops but they have to work out how the two ideas relate to each other and this can slow them down too.

Key words   sentence clause verb subject simple sentence
compound sentence conjunction complex sentence
main clause subordinate clause

Sentence types

Decide whether each of these sentences is simple, compound or complex.

1 It is cold tonight.

_____

2 While Dad was out, we baked his birthday cake.

_____

3 Eve stroked the cat and it purred happily.

_____

4 I wanted to buy some shoes but the shop had shut.

_____

5 We ran for the bus although it had already started moving.

_____

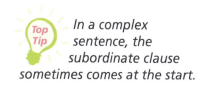

Top Tip In a complex sentence, the subordinate clause sometimes comes at the start.

5

Using sentence types

1 Give an example of how writers can use simple sentences successfully.

_____

_____

2 Write down one good and one bad effect that using compound or complex sentences can have on a reader.

Good _____

_____

Bad _____

_____

3

TOTAL MARKS 8

Contractions

Writing contractions

Contractions happen when two words are joined together, with one or more letters missing. The position of the missing letters is shown by an **apostrophe**.

I am = I'm	she is = she's
he will = he'll	they will = they'll
do not = don't	is not = isn't
I would = I'd	I have = I've

Most contractions are easy to write, but a few are harder. Sometimes letters are missed out in more than one place, or the letters are put in a different order!

will not = won't	shall not = shan't

please don't feed the monkeys

Using contractions

Contractions happen over time when we use two words together. We use them all the time when we talk to one another, but there are rules about using them in writing.

Contractions are great for bringing your characters' dialogue to life when you are writing stories. Writing **dialogue** the way people really speak makes it much more believable.

You can also use them for informal writing, like letters or emails to friends.

isearch

Hi Soph,

Can't wait to see you Sat night. I've got a fab new dress to wear. What are you wearing?

Hugs,
Hels x

Top Tip *Contractions should not be used in formal writing, like schoolwork or formal letters.*

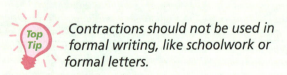

 Key words   contraction   apostrophe   dialogue

Writing contractions

This piece of writing contains **five** incorrectly spelt contractions. Can you underline them?

Dear Katie,

Hows your new home? We're really missing you at school. Your lucky

though because wer'e doing lots of tests this week. I cant believe it'll

be Christmas soon. You'l have to come and stay over the holidays.

Take care,

Beth

5

Using contractions

The writer of this formal letter has used contractions. Cross them out, then write the full forms in the spaces.

Dear Sirs,

I'm _____ writing to complain about the service we've

_____ received in your Newtown branch. We purchased a

kettle from the branch but when we got home we found that the lid

wasn't _____ in the box. The manager said she'd

_____ replace it but we haven't _____ heard

anything since then.

I would be grateful if you could look into the matter for me.

Yours faithfully,

M Dawson

5

TOTAL MARKS 10

Possessive apostrophes

Using possessive apostrophes

We can use **possessive apostrophes** to say that something belongs to someone or something.

When the person or thing an object belongs to is **singular**, you usually add an apostrophe then *s*.

    Sophie's watch   the squirrel's tail

If you are saying that an object belongs to more than one person and the word already ends in *s*, you usually just add an apostrophe without adding another *s*.

    two cats' tails   four boys' bags

Some **plural** nouns do not end in *s*. With these, you add an apostrophe, then *s*.

    the children's games   the people's hats

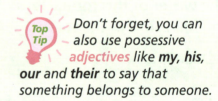

Top Tip *Don't forget, you can also use possessive **adjectives** like **my**, **his**, **our** and **their** to say that something belongs to someone.*

Its and it's

People often get mixed up between *its* and *it's*. You need to remember that *its* does not have an apostrophe when you are saying that something belongs to *it*.

    The flag fluttered on **its** pole.   The bird settled on **its** nest.

It's is the contracted form of *it is*.

    It's too late to play.   **It's** hot today.

 Key words   possessive apostrophe   singular   plural   adjective

LEARN

WRITING

Using possessive apostrophes

Write these sentences again, with the possessive apostrophes in the correct place.

1 The mens cars were parked side by side.

_____

2 The seals enclosure was next to the penguins.

_____

_____

3 The womens suitcases were stacked on a trolley.

_____

4 The two puppies tails waved wildly.

_____

_____

 Top Tip *The position of the possessive apostrophe is often the only way a reader can tell whether you are writing about one person, or more than one.*

4

Its and it's

Write two sentences using the word *its* and then two using *it's*.

1 _____

2 _____

3 _____

4 _____

4

TOTAL MARKS 8

Punctuation

LEARN

WRITING

Commas

Commas can be used to separate clauses in sentences. They tell readers when to pause, which helps them to understand the sentence properly.

In this complex sentence, a comma separates the main clause from the subordinate clause.

As she ran over, Katie shouted the exciting news.

Without the comma, it would sound like someone had run over Katie!

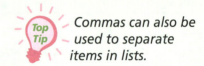

Top Tip **Commas can also be used to separate items in lists.**

Colons and semi-colons

Colons and **semi-colons** can both be used to organise sentences to make them easier to understand.

Semi-colons are used to separate clauses in sentences. Often they can be used to join two simple sentences together into one sentence.

I called my dog. He came running in.

I called my dog; he came running in.

Colons are used to introduce explanations or lists.

I was late for school. The bus was late.

I was late for school: the bus was late.

Parenthesis

Parenthesis is where words are added to a sentence in brackets to give the reader more information. Where you put the brackets is important. The sentence must make sense whether or not the reader reads the words in brackets.

The girl fell asleep.

The girl (who had been awake since early morning) fell asleep.

 Key words   comma   colon   semi-colon   parenthesis

Commas

Add the commas to these sentences.

1   My aunt who lives in Scotland is coming to stay next week.

2   When the film had finished we went out for pizza.

3   Anna Rachel Katie and Ruth sit on my table at school.

4   Yawning tiredly Mark went to bed.

4

Colons and semi-colons

Put a tick by a sentence that you think is true and a cross by one you think is false.

1   Colons can be used at the end of a sentence, instead of a full stop.

2   Colons can be used to introduce lists.

3   Semi-colons can sometimes be used to join two simple sentences.

4   Semi-colons can be used instead of speech marks.

4

Parenthesis

Underline the sentences in which the parenthesis has been used correctly.

1   I forgot my PE kit (again!).

2   My little brother rummaged (who is not allowed in my room) through my things.

3   (It started to rain) as we were walking home.

4   The car (which was very old) ground to a halt at the side of the road.

4

TOTAL MARKS 12

Writing about speech

Direct and reported speech

Reported speech is where the writer tells the reader about what someone has said, without using their exact words.

> The teacher told the class to be quiet.

It can be useful in stories because it allows you to write about what a character says without them having to be in the story at that point.

Direct speech is where the writer uses the actual words that someone says.
Speech marks show that someone is speaking and separates what they say from the rest of the sentence.

> "You're so cute!" whispered Claire.

Direct speech is brilliant for bringing your characters to life and letting them talk to each other.

 Top Tip *Use a combination of direct and reported speech in stories, as too much of either can make reading hard work.*

You're so cute!

Using dialogue to develop characters

When characters talk to each other, it is called dialogue. Real people talk all the time, so using dialogue is a brilliant way to develop realistic characters. Think about the kind of person your character is. Are they happy or sad? Kind or nasty? This will affect what they say and how they say it.

> The crazy inventor bounded across the room towards us. "**Hello**!" he **boomed, cheerfully**.

Try to avoid using the word *said* when you are introducing direct speech. Words like *asked, replied, argued* or *suggested* help to say lots more about how a character is speaking.

 Key words   reported speech   direct speech   speech marks

Direct and reported speech

1 Write this sentence again as reported speech.

"Shall we go shopping on Saturday?" suggested Mel.

_____

2 Write this sentence again as direct speech.

Mark explained that he was late because the bus had broken down.

_____

3 Write down one benefit of using direct speech.

_____

4 Write down one benefit of using reported speech.

_____

4

Using dialogue to develop characters

Choose the best ending for these sentences about characters from a story.
Underline your choices.

1 "I want it now!"

screamed the spoilt boy, rudely.

whispered the spoilt boy, shyly.

giggled the spoilt boy, excitedly.

2 "Cheer up!"

ordered the little girl, sharply.

shrieked the little girl, angrily.

coaxed the little girl, cheerfully.

2

TOTAL MARKS 6

Nouns and pronouns

Noun types

Nouns are words that name things.

Common nouns name ordinary things, e.g. shop, tree.

Proper nouns name people and places, and things like the days of the week and the months of the year. Proper nouns start with a capital letter wherever they appear in a sentence, e.g. Simon, Cornwall.

Abstract nouns name things that you can't touch or hold, like ideas or feelings, e.g. happiness, knowledge.

Top Tip
Collective nouns describe groups of things, e.g. a flock of sheep.

Pronouns

Pronouns like *I, me, she, he, they* and *us* can sometimes be used in place of nouns. They can save you from having to use the same noun again and again.

I tried to open the door, but **it** was stuck.

There are different pronouns to replace different nouns. Some help you to write about yourself, some are for males, some are for females and some are for groups of people.

Pronouns are really useful, but you need to use them with care.

The puppy chewed the slipper, so Dad threw it away.

Do you think Dad threw away the slipper or the puppy? It is impossible to be sure, because *it* could replace either noun!

Make sure the pronouns give enough information about what is happening in your sentences.

Key words noun   common noun   proper noun   abstract noun
collective noun   pronoun

Noun types

Write down **three** examples of each type of noun, for one mark each.

common noun	proper noun	abstract noun
_____	_____	_____
_____	_____	_____
_____	_____	_____

9

Pronouns

Add a suitable pronoun to complete each sentence.

1   Kathryn and Liz are my friends although _____ live far away.

2   When my baby sister starts crying, I know _____ is tired.

3   Dad ran after the dog but he couldn't catch _____.

3

TOTAL MARKS 12

Plurals

Spelling rules for plurals

Plural means more than one of a particular noun. Many plurals end in *s*.

shoes   gloves   socks

Singular nouns that end in *ss, sh, ch* or *x* end in *es* in the plural.

stitches   dishes   boxes

If the noun ends in a consonant then *y*, you must change the *y* to *ies*.

babies   ladies   jellies

With nouns that end in a consonant then *f*, you usually change the *f* to *ves*.

leaf   leaves

Top Tip *Words that end in **o** can be tricky. Most end in **es** in the plural, but some just end in **s** and some can have either ending. Check in a dictionary if you are not sure.*

Irregular plurals

Some nouns do not follow the rules when they become plurals. You need to learn these separately.

mouse   mice

child   children

person   people

Others are spelt the same, whether they are singular or plural.

fish   deer   sheep

 Key words   plural   singular

Spelling rules for plurals

Match up these word openings with the correct plural ending.

1	fox	es
2	train	eys
3	wol	s
4	pupp	ves
5	donk	ies
6	tomato	es

6

Irregular plurals

Write down the plurals of these nouns.

1 species _____

2 man _____

3 antelope _____

4 ox _____

5 woodlouse _____

6 tooth _____

6

TOTAL MARKS 12

Adjectives

Using adjectives

Adjectives describe nouns. Adjectives can help you to describe exactly what something is like. They can describe the size, shape and colour of something, how many there are, and who they belong to.

Try to avoid tired adjectives like *good*, *bad* or *big*, as there are many different ways something can be good, bad or big! Look for really powerful ones instead, that say more about the thing you are describing.

Huge, black clouds hung in the **gloomy** sky.

Comparative and superlative adjectives

Comparative adjectives allow you to compare two things.

My dog is **bigger** than yours.

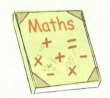

My maths homework is **more difficult** than my English work.

Superlative adjectives describe the most of a particular quality something can be.

My dog is the **biggest** of all.   It was the **most exciting** film I have ever seen.

Top Tip *Superlative adjectives are often used in persuasive writing, like adverts, e.g. the **latest** development in gaming.*

 Key words   adjective   comparative adjective   superlative adjective

Answers

PAGE 5

Planning for talking
Answers will vary.

Debating
Answers will vary, but one mark should be awarded for each point made.

Opinions
Answers will vary.

PAGE 7

The features of books
The covers of books include the name of the writer, or **author**, of the book as well as the name of the publisher. The back carries the **ISBN**, which is the book's unique identifying number. Inside, the **contents page** lists the chapters or sections in the book, while the index lists the topics alphabetically to help readers find what they need. The **glossary** lists useful or difficult words and is found at the back of some books.

The choices publishers make
Possible answers include:
1. A publisher might choose to present some information as bullet points because they are clear and easy to read quickly.
2. Some information is presented in boxes to draw the reader's attention to it.
3. Publishers sometimes include a glossary to explain technical or unfamiliar words to readers.

PAGE 9

Reading fiction
Answers will vary.

Reading non-fiction
Children should tick each feature as they find it.

PAGE 11

Reading techniques
1. non-fiction
2. It is about the opening of a new cinema complex.
3. Seaward
4. Because Seaward is a holiday resort, so there will be lots of holidaymakers driving around the town during the summer months.

Using deduction
1. The writer is old. We can tell this because they use the phrase 'those of us who remember', implying that they have lived in the town for a long time.

2. The writer may not like the changes that have happened in the town, so they see the cinema as being to blame for them.

PAGE 13

Authors
Answers will vary.

Narrator and viewpoint
Answers will vary, but should be written from the point of view of one of the ugly sisters and take into account the knowledge that the sisters have within the story.

PAGE 15

Biography
Possible answers include:
1. Biographies are written in the third person because they are written by a writer about the experiences of someone else.
2. A biography does not give a complete account of someone's life, because the biographer can never know every detail of their life.

Autobiography
Possible answers include:
1. Using the first person makes the reader feel that the writer is speaking directly to them.
2. Answers will vary.

PAGE 17

Sentence types
Simple sentence: 1
Compound sentences: 3, 4
Complex sentences: 2, 5

Using sentence types
Possible answers include:
1. Simple sentences can help to draw the reader's attention to really important pieces of information.
2. Good: Compound and complex sentences can help to combine ideas.
   Bad: They can slow the reader down, because they have to work out how the ideas relate to each other.

PAGE 19

Writing contractions
Dear Katie,

<u>Hows</u> your new home? We're really missing you at school. <u>Your</u> lucky though because

wer'e doing lots of tests this week. I <u>cant</u> believe it'll be Christmas soon. <u>You'l</u> have to come and stay over the holidays.

Take care,

Beth

Using contractions

Dear Sirs,

I am writing to complain about the service **we have** received in your Newtown branch. We purchased a kettle from the branch but when we got home we found that the lid **was not** in the box. The manager said **she would** replace it but we **have not** heard anything since then. I would be grateful if you could look into the matter for me.

Yours faithfully,

M Dawson

Using possessive apostrophes

1   The men's cars were parked side by side.
2   The seals' enclosure was next to the penguins.
3   The women's suitcases were stacked on a trolley.
4   The two puppies' tails waved wildly.

Its and it's

Answers will vary.

Commas

1   My aunt, who lives in Scotland, is coming to stay next week.
2   When the film had finished, we went out for pizza.
3   Anna, Rachel, Katie and Ruth sit on my table at school.
4   Yawning tiredly, Mark went to bed.

Colons and semi-colons

True: 2, 3
False: 1, 4

Parenthesis

Parenthesis has been used correctly in sentences 1 and 4.

Direct and reported speech

Possible answers include:

1   Mel suggested that we should go shopping on Saturday.
2   "I was late because the bus broke down," explained Mark.

3   Direct speech allows your characters to speak to each other, which makes them seem more realistic.
4   Reported speech allows you to write about what characters have said, without them actually being present in the story at that moment.

Using dialogue to develop characters

1   "I want it now!" screamed the spoilt boy, rudely.
2   "Cheer up!" coaxed the little girl, cheerfully.

Noun types

Possible answers include:

Common nouns: book, clock, house.
Proper nouns: Africa, Monday, Sarah.
Abstract nouns: joy, excitement, disappointment.

Pronouns

1   Kathryn and Liz are my friends although **they** live far away.
2   When my baby sister starts crying, I know **she** is tired.
3   Dad ran after the dog but he couldn't catch **it**.

Spelling rules for plurals

1   foxes
2   trains
3   wolves
4   puppies
5   donkeys
6   tomatoes

Irregular plurals

1   species
2   men
3   antelope or antelopes
4   oxen
5   woodlice
6   teeth

Using adjectives

Possible answers include:

1   A <u>tiny</u> bird sat on the <u>decaying</u> fence.
2   The <u>generous</u> girl gave her friend a <u>beautiful</u> present.
3   A <u>huge</u> storm blew <u>freezing</u> rain into our faces.
4   I was <u>exhausted</u> at the end of the race but <u>delighted</u> that I had won.

Comparative and superlative adjectives

	Comparative adjectives	Superlative adjectives
funny	**funnier**	funniest
flat	flatter	**flattest**
pretty	**prettier**	**prettiest**
expensive	**less expensive**	least expensive
exciting	more exciting	**most exciting**
generous	**more/less generous**	**most/least generous**

PAGE 33

Using verbs
Possible answers include:
1 said: announced, explained, replied
2 went: left, visited, travelled
3 ran: sprinted, jogged, raced

Verb tenses
1 Sam bought a newspaper.
2 Kate wrote a letter to her friend.
3 Chris and Daniel found a key on the pavement.

Active and passive verbs
Active sentences: 2, 3
Passive sentences: 1, 4

PAGE 35

Making adverbs work for you
Possible answers include:
1 "Who are you?" demanded the man, furiously.
2 Max gobbled the cake instantly.
3 Jane sauntered lazily in the sunshine.

Using adverbs
1 Bravely, the knight climbed the castle walls.
2 Carelessly, Gemma tore the paper off the present.
3 Furiously, Jake slammed the door.
4 Eventually, Tom found his football boots.

PAGE 37

Avoiding repetition
It was a hot day and we were soon hot and tired. We were all glad to reach the edge of the woodland and feel the cool woodland floor beneath our feet. As we began to pick a path through the trees, we began to hear the sounds of small creatures creeping through the undergrowth. As we got deeper into the forest, we started to feel afraid. We were afraid we would get lost, then Sam told us he had lost his compass!

Possible answers include:
1 warm
2 forest
3 started
4 scared
5 misplaced

Improving descriptions
1 Dad broke an egg into the cake mixture.
2 The rabbit hopped happily around its cage.
3 The hairdresser cut my hair.
4 The woman washed the little boy's dirty face.
5 Mum and I decorated the Christmas tree.

PAGE 39

Writing imagery
Possible answers include:
1 The wind struck the trees like a bulldozer.
2 The house was a lantern in the darkness.
3 The billowing laundry clung desperately to the line.

Avoiding clichés
1 The sun smiled down on the village.
   Possible alternatives include: The sun hung like a ball in the sky.
2 Our dog is as gentle as a lamb.
   Possible alternatives include: Our dog is like a playful child.
3 My science homework is a nightmare.
   Possible alternatives include: My science homework refuses to be conquered.

PAGE 41

Using alliteration and onomatopoeia
Answers will vary. Possible answers are:
1 I bobbed about blissfully.
2 The crockery shattered as it hit the floor.

Reading alliteration and onomatopoeia
Possible answers include:
1 The writer has used the phrase *padded past, huge paws pounding* because it is alliteration and it draws attention to the size of the tiger's paws.
2 The word *growling* describes the sound the tiger makes and it is onomatopoeia.

PAGE 43

The language of instructions
1 Allow 7 working days for your order to be processed.
2 Keep your receipt as proof of purchase.
3 Cut round your design with a craft knife.
4 Use an adjustable spanner to tighten the bolts.

Organising instructions
Answers will vary.

PAGE 45
Persuasive language
Answers will vary, but one mark should be awarded to each of the following features: a product name, a sentence about the benefits of the product, some factual information about price and availability, and a picture.

Understanding your reader
Red arguments: 3, 4, 6.
Blue arguments: 1, 2, 5.

PAGE 47
The language of recounts
Possible answers include:
We were watching TV when the lights suddenly went out. **First** Mum checked the fuse box, **before** looking outside to see if the neighbours' lights were out too. **When** she saw that nobody had any power, she found some candles. **After that** she found some torches. **Eventually** the power came back on.

Planning recounts
The three events that are not important enough to be included in a recount are:
7.50   He put on blue trousers.
7.55   He had toast for breakfast.
8.25   He found his old watch while he was looking.

PAGE 49
Understanding reports
The ideas that would not be included in the report are: medieval churches, Great Fire of London, World War II, Queen Victoria.

Report language
Answers will vary.

PAGE 51
Planning a story
Answers will vary.

Openings
Answers will vary.

Endings
Answers will vary.

PAGE 53
Developing characters
Answers will vary.

Describing settings
Answers will vary.

PAGE 55
Writing kennings poems
Possible answers include:
Shade-giver,
Log-maker,
Leaf-bearer,
Nest-hider,
Branch-waver.

Writing haiku
Possible answers include:
Summer
Sun shines in blue sky.
Corn waving in golden rows
Ready for harvest.
Autumn
Dry leaves fall softly.
Red orange yellow flurry;
Rich gold tapestry.
Winter
Pale sun in grey sky.
Frost sparkles on bare branches;
Snow clouds gathering.

Letts Educational
4 Grosvenor Place, London SW1X 7DL
School enquiries: 015395 64911/65921
Parent & student enquiries: 015395 64913
E-mail: mail@lettsandlonsdale.co.uk

Website: www.letts-educational.com

First published 2008

Editorial and design: 2ibooks [publishing solutions] Cambridge

Author: Alison Head
Book concept and development: Helen Jacobs, Publishing Director
Editorial: Sophie London, Senior Commissioning Editor
       Katy Knight, Editorial Assistant
Illustrators: Andy Roberts and Phillip Burrows
Cover design: Angela English

Letts & Lonsdale make every effort to ensure all paper used in our books is made from wood pulp obtained from sustainable and well-managed forests. Every effort has been made to trace copyright holders and obtain their permission for the use of copyright material. The authors and publishers will gladly receive information enabling them to rectify any error or omission in subsequent editions. All facts are correct at time of going to press.

All our Rights Reserved. No part of the publication may be produced, stored in a retrieval system, or transmitted, in any form or by any means, electronic, mechanical, photocopying, recording or otherwise, without the prior permission of Letts Educational.

British Library Cataloging in Publication Data. A CIP record of this book is available from the British Library.

ISBN 9781843158790

Text, design and illustration © Letts Educational Limited 2008

Printed in Italy

Using adjectives

Write these sentences again, with more powerful adjectives replacing the bold words.

1 A **small** bird sat on the **old** fence.

_____

2 The **kind** girl gave her friend a **nice** present.

_____

3 A **big** storm blew **cold** rain into our faces.

_____

4 I was **tired** at the end of the race but **pleased** that I had won.

_____

_____

8

Comparative and superlative adjectives

Fill in this chart with the missing words.

	Comparative adjectives	Superlative adjectives
funny		funniest
flat	flatter	
pretty		
expensive		least expensive
exciting	more exciting	
generous		

 Top Tip _When you add the **er** suffix to words, you often have to change the spelling of the root word first._

8

TOTAL MARKS 16

Verbs

Using verbs

Verbs describe actions. Every sentence must have a verb, but that doesn't mean you have to keep using the same ones again and again. Try to pick verbs that describe exactly what a person or thing is doing.

The cat **walked** up to the bird.   The cat **crept** up to the bird.

Look for interesting verbs, which say more about the action.

walked ➜ sauntered   said ➜ explained   went ➜ travelled

Verb tenses

Verbs change their **tense** to tell us whether something has already happened, is happening now, or will happen in the future.

I swam in a competition. (**past tense**)

I am swimming in a competition. (**present tense**)

I shall swim in a competition. (**future tense**)

Lots of past tense verbs end in *ed*, but many are completely different in the past tense.

is ➜ was   bring ➜ brought   lose ➜ lost   eat ➜ ate

Active and passive verbs

Verbs can be active or passive.
Active verbs tell us about something   The dog ate its biscuits.
that a person or thing is doing.

Sentences that contain a **passive verb** tell us about what is being done, but might not always tell us who or what is doing the action.

The door was slammed shut in my face.

We know what happened to the door, but not who slammed it!

Key words   tense   past tense   present tense   future tense
active verb   passive verb

Using verbs

Think of three verbs you could use instead of each of these verbs.

1 said _____ _____ _____

2 went _____ _____ _____

3 ran _____ _____ _____

9

Verb tenses

Write these present tense sentences again, in the past tense.

1 Sam buys a newspaper.

_____

2 Kate writes a letter to her friend.

_____

3 Chris and Daniel find a key on the pavement.

_____

 Top Tip *Some verbs stay the same in the present tense and the past tense, e.g.* **read**, **hit**, **cut**, **hurt**.

3

Active and passive verbs

Decide whether you think each sentence contains an active or a passive verb. Write A for active or P for passive in each box.

1 The boy was taken to hospital. ☐

2 The baby threw its rattle across the room. ☐

3 The bird caught a worm. ☐

4 The window was suddenly broken. ☐

4

TOTAL MARKS 16

Adverbs

Making adverbs work for you

Adverbs are words that describe verbs.
They allow you to say more about how an action takes place.

The wind blew **gently**.

The wind blew **fiercely**.

Many adverbs end in *ly*. In fact, a lot of them are made by adding *ly* to an adjective.

silent + ly = silently

Other adverbs have different endings.
Very, here and *there* are all adverbs too.

Teaming up the right adverb with a really powerful verb can transform your writing.

She walked angrily out of the room.

She stormed furiously out of the room.

Which sentence paints a more vivid picture?

Using adverbs

Verbs can be used without adverbs, but every adverb needs a verb to work with.

Most of the time, the verb comes first, followed by the adverb.

The girls whispered secretively.

verb   adverb

Sometimes, though, adverbs can work really well at the start of a sentence. This works brilliantly when the way in which an action takes place is the most important thing in the sentence.

Suddenly, the door burst open.

adverb   verb

 Key words   adverb

Making adverbs work for you

Improve each sentence by replacing the blue verb and the green adverb with more interesting alternatives. Write the new sentences.

The teacher spoke nicely to the children.

The teacher chatted kindly to the children.

1 "Who are you?" asked the man, crossly.

_____

2 Max ate the cake quickly.

_____

3 Jane walked slowly in the sunshine.

_____

3

Using adverbs

Write these sentences again, with the red adverb at the beginning.

Sarah greeted her cousin shyly.   Shyly, Sarah greeted her cousin.

1 The knight bravely climbed the castle walls.

_____

2 Gemma carelessly tore the paper off the present.

_____

3 Jake slammed the door furiously.

_____

4 Tom found his football boots eventually.

_____

4

Synonyms

Avoiding repetition

Synonyms are words with similar meanings. We can use them to avoid having to repeat the same word in our writing.

> The cat **walked** along the fence, jumped down and **walked** into the house.

The repetition in this sentence is rather boring. Replacing one or both of the bold words will make it sound better.

> The cat **crept** along the fence, jumped down and **stalked** into the house.

Read your writing through carefully, to see if you need to find synonyms for words you have repeated.

Improving descriptions

Synonyms can also help us to describe things in better detail. This is because not all synonyms have exactly the same meaning. Choosing the correct one for each sentence will make your writing much more interesting to read.

> The squirrel **ran** across the lawn towards the tree and the dog **ran** after it.

In this sentence, both animals are running. Squirrels and dogs run in very different ways though, so replacing the verb 'ran' with carefully chosen synonyms will avoid repetition and give the sentence more meaning.

> The squirrel **scampered** across the lawn towards the tree and the dog **tore** after it.

Top Tip *Synonyms can help you to write great poetry, because you can pick a synonym with the right number of syllables, or one which rhymes with another word.*

 Key words   synonym   thesaurus

Avoiding repetition

Read this piece of writing through and underline words that you would replace with synonyms, to avoid repetition. Write the new words you would use on the lines below.

It was a hot day and we were soon hot and tired. We were all glad to reach the edge of the woodland and feel the cool woodland floor beneath our feet. As we began to pick a path through the trees, we began to hear the sounds of small creatures creeping through the undergrowth. As we got deeper into the forest, we started to feel afraid. We were afraid we would get lost, then Sam told us he had lost his compass!

1 _____   4 _____

2 _____   5 _____

3 _____

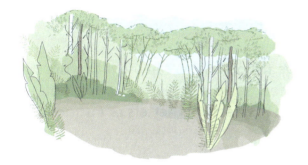

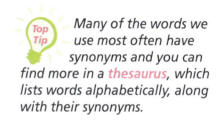 *Many of the words we use most often have synonyms and you can find more in a thesaurus, which lists words alphabetically, along with their synonyms.*

Top Tip

5

Improving descriptions

Choose the best synonym to complete each sentence. Cross out the words you reject.

1   Dad (shattered   smashed   broke) an egg into the cake mixture.

2   The rabbit (jumped   hopped   leapt) happily around its cage.

3   The hairdresser (cut   sliced   chopped) my hair.

4   The woman (laundered   washed   hosed) the little boy's dirty face.

5   Mum and I (embellished   enhanced   decorated) the Christmas tree.

5

TOTAL MARKS 10

Imagery

Writing imagery

Imagery is the name given to creative writing techniques that help to build up a picture for your readers. There are three main types you can use.

Simile is a way of comparing one thing with another, using the words *as* or *like*.

> Cherries shone like jewels in the branches of the trees.

Metaphor is where you say that an object is something else.

> The mountain was a sleeping giant.

Personification is where a non-human thing is described using human characteristics.

> Huge fir trees stood guard by the gate to the castle.

Imagery is perfect for writing really effective fiction, as you can use it to write strong descriptions of the way things look, sound, feel, taste or smell. You would not normally use it in non-fiction writing like reports, recounts, letters or instructions.

Top Tip: *If you are asked to write about a piece of text that someone else has written, be sure to comment on how they have used imagery.*

Avoiding clichés

There are lots of well-known similes and metaphors that we use all the time when we are speaking. These are called **clichés**.

> as pretty as a picture   a wolf in sheep's clothing

Most people have heard phrases like this lots of times before, so they can sound a bit boring if they are used in writing. Have a go at writing your own imagery instead.

 Key words   imagery   simile   metaphor   personification   cliché

LEARN | WRITING

Writing imagery

Look at the picture, then answer the questions.

1   Write a sentence containing a simile to describe the weather in the picture.

_____

2   Write a sentence containing a metaphor to describe the house.

_____

3   Write a sentence containing personification to describe the washing on
    the line.

_____

_____

3

Avoiding clichés

Underline the clichés in these sentences. Then write the
sentences again, using your own imagery.

1   The sun smiled down on the village.

_____

2   Our dog is as gentle as a lamb.

_____

3   My science homework is a nightmare.

_____

3

TOTAL MARKS   6

Special effects

Using alliteration and onomatopoeia

Good writers use the way words sound to create powerful effects in their writing.

Alliteration is where words that start with the same sound are used together. When they are read out, the repeated sound helps to draw your reader's attention to that part of the writing.

> Looking up, Simon saw a spider on the ceiling.

> The rabbit hopped into the wood, followed by the furtive fox.

Onomatopoeia is where words sound like the things they describe.

> Frogs **croaked** from the river bank.

> The baby **wailed** in its pram.

An onomatopoeic word allows you to describe what something sounds like in a single word.

Top Tip *You will need to use your knowledge of synonyms to find words with the right meaning that start with the correct sound.*

Reading alliteration and onomatopoeia

In reading tests, you will often be asked why you think a writer has used a particular phrase. To get full marks, you need to say what type of technique has been used and what effect it creates.

> The writer has used alliteration to emphasise how strong the wind is. Repeating the 'w' sound also draws attention to the whistling sound of the wind.

The wind wailed and whipped through the trees, tearing at the branches. Above the noise of the storm came a cracking sound followed by a scraping, as the shed roof was torn loose and dragged along the garden path.

> The writer has used onomatopoeia to help the reader to imagine the sound of the shed roof blowing off and the damage that has been done.

Key words   alliteration   onomatopoeia

Using alliteration and onomatopoeia

1 Imagine you are rocking in a rowing boat on a calm sea. Use alliteration to write a sentence describing what it is like.

_____

2 Imagine you are carrying a tray of china cups and plates. You trip and drop the tray. Write a sentence using onomatopoeia to describe the sound it makes.

_____

2

Reading alliteration and onomatopoeia

Read the text, then answer the questions.

> We went to see the tigers next. One of the males padded past, huge paws pounding in the dust. He turned and faced us, baring his sharp teeth and growling.

1 Why has the writer used the phrase _padded past, huge paws pounding_?

_____

2 Why do you think the writer has used the word _growling_?

_____

2

TOTAL MARKS 4

Instructions

The language of instructions

Instructions do not ask you to do something, they tell you! They do this by using the **imperative**. That means that they use the verb first, without using a noun or pronoun before it.

Draw around a circular plate.

Cut carefully around the circle.

In any other kind of writing, ordering people around like this would seem rude! It works in instructions, however, because it makes the reader focus on what they need to do.

Instructions often contain technical vocabulary and may contain specific information, like numbers, to tell the reader how many or how much of a particular thing the reader needs to use.

Use a **balloon whisk** to whip **two** egg whites.

It is important to get details like this correct, or the instructions might not work.

Organising instructions

Instructions break a task down into small steps that are described chronologically. It is usually very important that the tasks are carried out in the correct order, so they are often numbered to make sure.

They might also contain time connectives to tell the reader when to do each step.

Once the egg whites are soft and fluffy, fold in the sugar.

Bake in a hot oven **until** the meringue is golden brown.

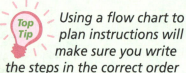

Top Tip

Using a flow chart to plan instructions will make sure you write the steps in the correct order and don't miss anything out.

Key words   imperative

The language of instructions

Write these sentences again, using the imperative to turn them into instructions.

1   You need to allow 7 working days for your order to be processed.

_____

2   You should keep your receipt as proof of purchase.

_____

Underline the technical vocabulary used in these sentences.

3   Cut round your design with a craft knife.

4   Use an adjustable spanner to tighten the bolts.

4

Organising instructions

Think about where you are sitting now. Write four numbered instructions to tell someone else how to get to the nearest door.

1   _____

2   _____

3   _____

4   _____

4

Persuasive writing

Persuasive language

Persuasive writing like adverts and brochures uses powerful language to build up a convincing argument for why the reader should buy a product, visit an attraction or adopt a particular point of view.

Most persuasive writing uses very few words, so each one must work hard to persuade the reader. Adverts often use superlative adjectives to make the product, place or idea sound like the best choice. Powerful adjectives help to create the idea that it is good value, or exciting in some way.

   The highest, fastest white-knuckle ride on the planet.

Persuasive writing often doesn't need to be written in full sentences. Give it a strong title, then use bullet points, boxed text and sub-headings. Don't forget to think about any factual information you need to include, like prices, addresses and dates.

Understanding your reader

The key to successful persuasive writing is to understand the audience you are writing for. You need to build up a convincing argument that will appeal to your reader.

For example, if you were writing a leaflet about a holiday park designed for adults wanting to book a holiday, you would probably emphasise things like value for money and convenience. If the leaflet was for a child, you might write about all the sports on offer and the huge ice cream parlour.

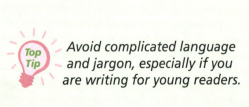
Avoid complicated language and jargon, especially if you are writing for young readers.

Persuasive language

Design a leaflet to advertise a new chocolate bar that does not melt in warm weather. You will gain one mark each for including a product name, a sentence about the benefits of the product, some factual information about price and availability, and a suitable picture.

Top Tip *In a test you will not get any extra marks for drawing pictures on leaflets or posters if they have not been asked for.*

4

Understanding your reader

Here are some arguments you could use to promote a new brand of bike. Colour the three arguments red that would be more likely to appeal to people your age. Colour the three arguments blue that would appeal to adults.

1   The bikes are great value for money.

2   The bikes are the safest on the market.

3   The bikes come in a wide range of colours.

4   You can buy lots of cool accessories for the bikes.

5   The seats and handlebars are adjustable, so the bikes will last a long time.

6   Several celebrities own one.

6

TOTAL MARKS   10

Recounts

The language of recounts

Recounts tell the reader about something that has happened. A recount could be a piece of biography or autobiography about a historical event, or an account of a school trip or holiday.

Recounts are written in the past tense, with the events described in chronological order. They are often linked together with time connectives, which help to make the order of events clearer.

> **When** Mum was wrapping the presents we had to go upstairs. **Later,** we crept downstairs to see if we could work out what was inside them.

You might have to describe things quite carefully, but because recounts are non-fiction, they shouldn't contain imagery like simile, metaphor and personification.

Planning recounts

Recounts are quite easy to write, especially if you plan them carefully. Try using a time line or flow chart to list all of the main events in the correct order. It will save you time by making sure you write about them in the right order, without missing anything out.

Think carefully about which events to include in your recount. In a test you probably won't have time to describe every little thing that happened. Instead, pick the main events that influenced the outcome and leave out anything insignificant.

Key words recount

The language of recounts

Add suitable time connectives to complete this recount.

We were watching TV when the lights suddenly went out.

_____ Mum checked the fuse box, _____ looking

outside to see if the neighbours' lights were out too. _____

she saw that nobody had any power, she found some candles.

_____ she found some torches. _____ the power

came back on.

5

Planning recounts

Read the time line and decide which events are important enough to be included in a recount and which are not. Cross out the three you would **not** include. You will get a mark for each of them.

7.30 — Philip got up to get ready for his holiday.

7.50 — He put on blue trousers.

7.55 — He had toast for breakfast.

8.15 — He could not find his passport.

8.25 — He found his old watch while he was looking.

8.50 — He found the passport.

9.55 — He arrived at the airport, just in time.

3

TOTAL MARKS 8

Reports

Understanding reports

A **report** is a piece of factual writing about a particular subject. Information in reports is organised into topics, rather than chronologically.

Research your topic in books and on the Internet. Remember that there will be thousands of facts about your subject. It is your job to pick the ones that are most relevant to the report you are writing. For example, if you were writing a report about working children in the Victorian age, there would be no point including information about Victorian buildings, no matter how interesting you found it.

Once you have collected your ideas, use a spidergram or tree diagram to help you group similar ideas together in sections. Then work out how the different themes of each section connect to each other and put them in order. Then simply write a paragraph for each section of your plan.

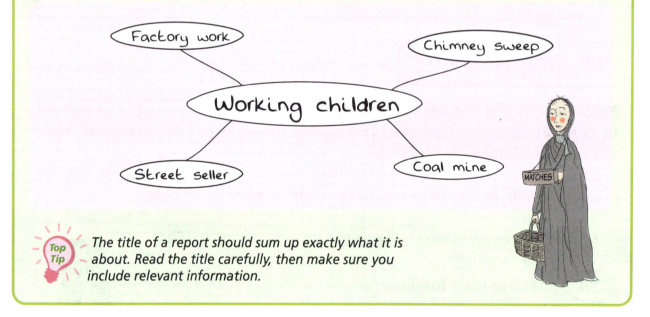

Top Tip *The title of a report should sum up exactly what it is about. Read the title carefully, then make sure you include relevant information.*

Report language

Reports are often written in the present tense, unless they are about a historical period.

They are non-fiction and fairly formal, so don't use imagery, slang or contractions. Think about whether you need to use any technical vocabulary that goes with the subject. For example, if you were writing a report about car engines, you might need to use terms like *distributor cap* and *head gasket*.

Key words report

Understanding reports

Look carefully at this spidergram. Some of the ideas are not relevant to the title of the report, which is in the middle. Cross out the four ideas that you would **not** include in a report.

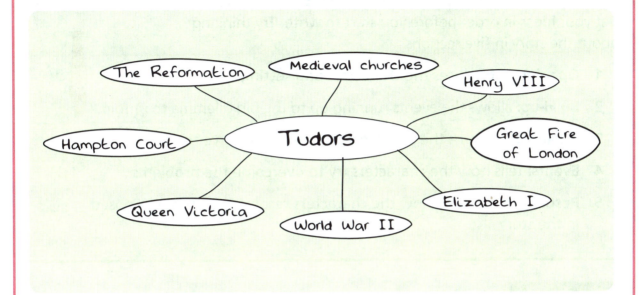

4

Report language

Imagine you are writing a short report to tell your classmates about a sport or hobby you enjoy. Write four sentences of your report, using appropriate language.

_____

_____

_____

_____

_____

_____

_____

4

TOTAL MARKS 8

Planning stories

Planning a story

LEARN

WRITING

Planning a story will save you time in a test, by helping you to get your ideas in order before you start to write. Try thinking about the story in five sections.

1   **Opening:** introduces the characters and settings.

2   **Build-up:** allows the events running up to the big dilemma to unfold.

3   **Dilemma:** explains the problems the characters have to overcome.

4   **Events:** tells how the characters try to overcome the problems.

5   **Resolution:** explains how the characters resolve the problems posed in the story.

Openings

The best openings hook the reader straight away, with powerful descriptive words and lots of action. Try leaving a question unanswered in the first few sentences, so the reader has to keep reading to find out what happens next.

 Try starting a story with one of your characters speaking, or a description of the setting or a character.

Endings

Decide how your story ends before you start writing, so you can build up to the ending as you write. Try to leave your reader with something to think about after they have finished reading.

Here are some ideas for story endings.

• **Happy ending.**

• **Moral ending:** one of the characters learns a lesson.

• **Cliff-hanger:** characters are left in a dangerous situation with no obvious way out.

• **Twist in the tale:** something unexpected happens right at the end.

Planning a story

On with the show! A group of children plan a fundraising show to save a rundown local theatre, but things quickly get out of hand when the theatre's ghostly inhabitants join the cast.

Write a short plan for this story, in five sections.

Opening: _____

Build-up: _____

Dilemma: _____

Events: _____

Resolution: _____

5

Openings

Write the first four sentences of the story.

_____

_____

_____

_____

4

Endings

Write a sentence that explains what kind of ending you have chosen for the story and why you made that choice.

_____

_____

1

Characters and settings

Developing characters

Creating believable, realistic characters is the best way to hook your reader. Think about what each character would behave, sound and look like if they were real. If you spend time developing characters before you start writing, they will seem real right from the start.

Think about the role that each character will play in the plot and try to develop their personalities to fit. So if a character goes on a dangerous journey later in the story, make them seem brave and strong right from the start.

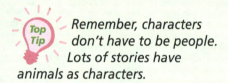 *Remember, characters don't have to be people. Lots of stories have animals as characters.*

Describing settings

The setting is the place where your story happens. Use imagery like simile, metaphor and personification to help your reader to imagine what your settings look, sound, smell and feel like. Match the setting to the feeling in the story at that moment and use imagery to create the right atmosphere.

You can have more than one setting in a story, especially if you need to change the feel of the story in the middle. Use connective phrases like *meanwhile, back in the mine,* or *later, at home* to move between settings, so your reader knows where the action is taking place. Try not to hop between locations too often, or your reader won't be able to keep up!

Developing characters

Imagine you are writing a story about two children who live in neighbouring houses. One is friendly, honest and reliable. The other is dishonest, spiteful and unfriendly. Write contrasting character profiles, for five marks each.

Character 1

Name: _____

Age: _____

Appearance: _____

_____

Behaviour: _____

_____

Special words and phrases to describe them:

_____

_____

Character 2

Name: _____

Age: _____

Appearance: _____

_____

Behaviour: _____

_____

Special words and phrases to describe them:

_____

_____

10

Describing settings

Now think about how the settings that the characters live in could emphasise their personalities. Jot down three creative words or phrases you could use to describe each character's house.

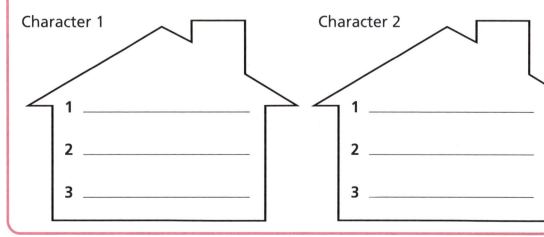

Character 1

1 _____

2 _____

3 _____

Character 2

1 _____

2 _____

3 _____

6

TOTAL MARKS 16

Poetry

Writing kennings poems

A **kenning** is a way of describing something without saying what it is. You can make a kennings poem by joining together several kennings about the same thing. They are interesting because the reader has to piece together the different descriptions to work out what the poem is about. Verbs are usually very important in kennings poems, so make sure you pick good ones.

Age-counter,

Candle-lighter,

Card-sender,

Present-bringer,

Party-thrower.

> **Top Tip** *Try adding extra impact by turning your poem into a* **calligram***, where the shape of the writing itself suits the subject of the poem.* **SCARY**, **historical**, **funny!**

What do you think this kennings poem is about?

Writing haiku

A **haiku** is a type of Japanese poem.

Haiku always have 17 **syllables**, organised in the same way. Count the syllables in each line.

First line: 5 syllables.   Tiny ladybird,

Second line: 7 syllables.   Balances on blades of grass:

Third line: 5 syllables.   Then she flies away.

Haiku are very short, so they tend to be used to describe small but beautiful details, like a dewy spider's web or a pearly seashell.

Traditionally, they often contained a clue to the season they were about. The poet might mention snow for winter, blossom for spring, a mosquito for summer and falling leaves for autumn.

> **Top Tip** *Remember, a syllable is a beat in a word. Fly has one syllable, beetle has two, dragonfly has three.*

Key words   **kenning**   **calligram**   **haiku**   **syllable**

LEARN

WRITING

Writing kennings poems

Write a five-line kennings poem about trees.

_____

_____

_____

_____

_____

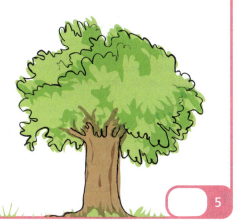

5

Writing haiku

Read this haiku about spring, then complete the seasons by writing haiku for Summer, Autumn and Winter.

Spring

Blossom on branches,

Pink petals blown on the wind;

Summer is coming.

Summer

_____

_____

_____

Autumn

_____

_____

_____

Winter

_____

_____

_____

3

TOTAL MARKS   8

Glossary

abstract noun a noun that names a feeling or idea, e.g. happiness, sorrow

active verb a verb that describes who is doing the action, e.g. Eve ate the sweets.

adjective a word or phrase that describes a noun

adverb a word or phrase that describes a verb

alliteration a phrase where most or all of the words begin with the same sound

apostrophe a punctuation mark used for contraction, when two words are joined, or to show possession, e.g. We'll collect Dad's car.

author the person who writes a text

autobiography the story of someone's life that they write themselves

biography the story of someone's life written by someone else

blurb information on the back of a book designed to give the reader an idea of what it is about

calligram a poem written in a typeface which demonstrates the theme of the poem

clause a distinct part of a sentence including a verb

cliché a word or phrase that has been overused for so long that people have grown tired of it

collective noun a name for a group of things, e.g. a swarm of flies

colon a punctuation mark that can be used to introduce explanations or lists

comma a punctuation mark that shows when to pause, separates clauses, or separates items in a list

common noun a noun that names ordinary things, e.g. book, car

comparative adjective an adjective that allows you to compare two things, e.g. smaller, less exciting

complex sentence a sentence that contains a main clause and a subordinate clause

compound sentence a sentence that contains two equally weighted clauses, joined together with a conjunction

conjunction a word used to link sentences or clauses, or to connect words within a phrase, e.g. so, and, later

contraction when words are shortened, or two words are joined, by removing letters and replacing with an apostrophe, e.g. can't, won't

deduction the ability to use clues in the text to understand its hidden meanings

dialogue a spoken or written conversation between two people

direct speech words that are actually spoken, enclosed in speech marks

empathy the ability to understand the feelings and motivations of the characters in stories

fiction stories with imaginary characters, settings or events

first person events told in the first person are told from the viewpoint of the person doing an action, e.g. I am playing chess.

future tense describes things that will happen in the future

glossary a collection of useful words and their meanings

haiku a Japanese poem containing 17 syllables

imagery words used to build up a picture in a story, including simile, metaphor and personification

imperative a way of using verbs to give an order or instruction, e.g. Turn left at the traffic lights.

ISBN a unique number on the back of a book used by booksellers and libraries

kenning a way of describing a thing without naming it

main clause the main part of a sentence which makes sense on its own

metaphor where a writer describes something as if it were something else, e.g. The bird was an arrow, tearing across the sky.

narrator the person from whose viewpoint a story is told. May or may not be a character in the story

non-fiction writing that is not fictional, including information texts about real people and places, letters, instructions and reports

noun a word that names a thing or feeling

onomatopoeia when a word sounds like the noise it describes, e.g. crash, shatter

opinion what someone thinks or believes

parenthesis words added to a sentence in brackets to add extra information

passive verb a verb that describes the actions rather than the person acting, e.g. The room was tidied by Dan.

past tense describes things that have already happened

personification a writing technique in which human characteristics are used to describe non-human things, e.g. Shadows crept across the floor.

plural more than one of something, usually made by adding s or es, e.g. dogs, dresses

possessive apostrophe an apostrophe used to show that something belongs to someone, e.g. Sarah's homework

present tense describes things that are happening now

pronoun a word used instead of a noun to avoid having to use the same noun again, e.g. I, she, we, me

proper noun a noun that names a specific person, thing or place, e.g. Chris, Manchester, Friday

recount a report that describes events in chronological order, or the order in which they happened

report an information text about a particular subject

reported speech speech reported in a text, but not directly quoted, e.g. She said she was tired.

scan read quickly to find a specific piece of information

semi-colon a punctuation mark used to join clauses in a sentence where one adds information to the other

sentence a unit of text that makes sense on its own

simile where a writer compares one thing with another, using the words as or like, e.g. as bold as brass

simple sentence a sentence containing one clause

singular one of something, e.g. a bird

skim read quickly to understand the main meaning of a piece of text

speech marks punctuation marks that surround direct speech. Other punctuation goes inside them, e.g. "Goodbye," said Mum.

subject the person or thing in a sentence that carries out the action, e.g. Amy bit the apple.

subordinate clause a clause which adds extra information to the main clause, but does not make sense on its own

superlative adjective an adjective that describes the most of a particular quality that something can be, e.g. fastest, least expensive

syllable a beat within a word, e.g. di-no-saur

synonym a word with exactly or nearly the same meaning as another word, e.g. hot, warm

tense tells us when something is happening

thesaurus a book of synonyms

third person events told in the third person are told from the viewpoint of someone other than the person doing an action, e.g. She is working hard today.

verb a doing or being word, e.g. walk, sleep

viewpoint how a story is told from a specific character's way of looking at things